WISDOM

And

Writings

Tracey Payton Younger

WISDOM

And

Writings

Tracey Payton Younger

WRITE THE VISION INTERNATIONAL PRESS

Published by Write The Vision International Press

www.TraceyPaytonYounger.com

YoungerTraceyP@gmail.com

267.283.0172

This book is dedicated in memory of my grandmother, Agnes Gilbert Barton, whom we all called "Sister". She always had words of wisdom and encouragement for me. I know that her prayers and what she had sown into my life has blessed me to be the woman I am now and am still yet becoming. Her legacy will live on.

ACKNOWLEDGEMENTS

When you start to thank people, you can possibly end up with an incredibly long list and or leave someone out. So, I would like to begin by thanking the Lord for walking me through this new venture. There were many times I lost my focus and was ready to give up, because of "lack", but the Lord would always send me a Word of encouragement and confirmation to get me moving again. I know it is because of Him, I am able to present this book to you.

I want to thank my true friends and all of you who have been active supporters of me. I thank the Lord that He has placed you in my life. You inspire and motivate me as I am privileged to watch you move and strive in your own lives. It has been a wonderful experience seeing you grow and sharing in your successes. I am honored to be able to help you along your journey. Thank you for being the Encouragers, the Inspirers, the Cheerleaders, the Motivators, the Gentle Correctors, in my life. Your lives and actions have inspired these writings. I love and appreciate you so much!

A special thank you to my family: Mommy, Diana, Michael, Yvonne, George and Nicholas. Thank you for your love and support. Even though there are times you may not understand my ways or why I do what I do, you still keep loving me and walking with me. I thank God for giving me such a wonderful loving family. I love You!

To my 'bestest' friend, Tamara. You are "a true friend". We have laughed together, cried together, prayed together, been through so much together and we are still here! Hallelujah! You have truly loved me through the good, the bad, the beautiful and the ugly. It has been a privilege and honor to walk alongside you and to see you continually grow into being "God's Woman." You have such a big heart and you give so much to help others. You inspire me! I love you, my Sister!

To my brother and friend, Darryl. It seems like I have known you for years, but it has only been a short time. I truly thank the Lord for you! You have been such an inspiration to me and have impacted my life immensely. Being in your company has pushed me to be better. It is rare to see a "real man" who is truly living for the Lord. Your example is a wonderful reflection of the Savior. Thank you for all of your encouragement, words of wisdom and gentle correction. Thank you for all that you have poured into my life. I love you, my Brother!

To Bishop David G. Evans. Thank you for your tireless labor in teaching us the Word and insuring that we have the tools to live by. I love your excitement as you impart wisdom and knowledge to us. Thank you for always encouraging us not to allow what we see to limit what we can do. Love you Bishop!

A NOTE TO YOU

The words I have written and the scriptures I have chosen are from my heart to inspire, to encourage, and to motivate you to move to another, deeper level in your life, in Jesus. Do not stay stuck in the same position. Familiar and comfortable are not always what is best for us. If you truly love and are in love with Jesus, then strive to be more like Him. If you are earnestly seeking and growing in Him, there will be noticeable changes in your life. Do people say, "You haven't changed one bit.", or do they remark, "Wow! You have really changed!"? I know about comfort zones all too well. There were various times in my life where I found myself in the same situation for a long period of time. Where I had snuggled up and settled into my circumstances like an old, worn out, favorite blanket. Although, I would be stuck in the situation for a moment, an urgency would arise within me to keep moving. Even though at times my response may have been slow, I still moved. I thank the Holy Spirit for that. So, I encourage you to move into that new place of new beginnings and expectations in Christ Jesus. Just trust Him with every aspect of your life and I guarantee, He will not fail you for there is no failure in Him.

In His Service,

Trai'

POETRY & WRITING TITLES

His Word

A Man Of Integrity

Strength

A True Sister

Know Your Worth

You Are On His Mind

To The Fathers

To The Mothers

Remember When...

Do Not Fear

Do Not Worry

Changing Venues

A New Thing

Continue

Trust And Honor Him

Successful Living

Discernment

Friendship

Loss

Positive Thinking

The Unbreakable Bond

Faith

Impartation

Assurance

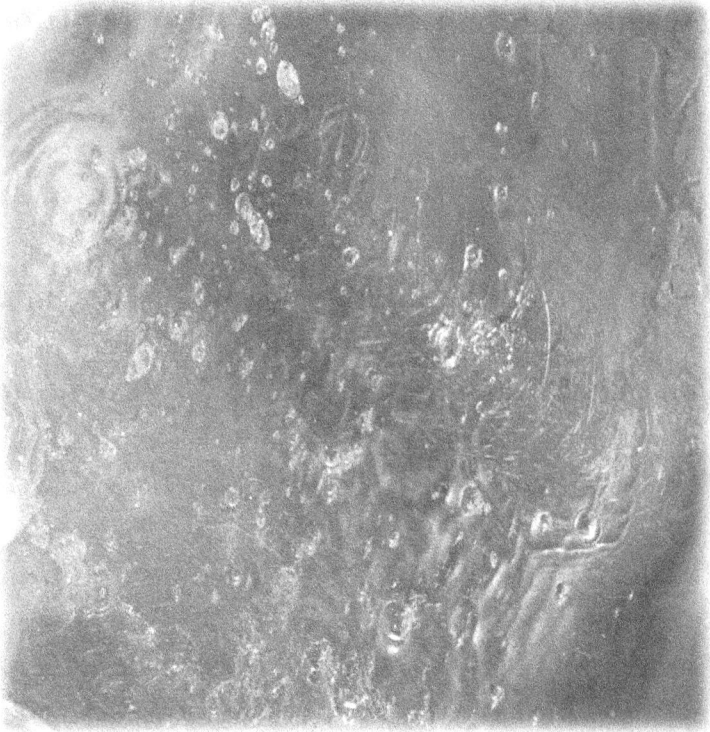

HIS WORD

This book of the law shall not depart out of thy mouth; but thou shalt meditate therein day and night, that thou mayest observe to do according to all that is written therein: for then thou shalt make thy way prosperous, and then thou shalt have good success.

Blessed is the man that walketh not in the counsel of the ungodly, nor standeth in the way of sinners, nor sitteth in the seat of the scornful. But his delight is in the law of the LORD; and in His law doth he meditate day and night. And he shall be like a tree planted by the rivers of water, that bringeth forth his fruit in his season; his leaf also shall not wither; and whatsoever he doeth shall prosper.

Wherewithal shall a young man cleanse his way? By taking heed thereto according to Thy word. With my whole heart have I sought Thee: O let me not wander from Thy commandments. Thy word have I hid in mine heart, that I might not sin against Thee.

Scripture References: Joshua 1:8; Psalm 1:1-3; Psalm 119:9-11

A MAN OF INTEGRITY

You are a wonderful reflection of Christ.

The Word, Wisdom, and your Wit are attractive
qualities that you possess.

You are Kind, Gentle, Sweet, and Patient.

You bear the fruit of Self-Control in abundance.

Through your adversities, you hold tight to your joy,
which shines through in the encouragement that you
give to others.

You think outside the box.

You walk with confidence due to your deep Faith in
God. It is contagious and motivates others to move
from their place of comfort.

You invest time and share your gifts and talents with
others.

In LOVE, you dispense correction.

God has Anointed you to accomplish all that He has
predestinated you to achieve in Him.

You are truly a man of God.

We see the Jesus in you!

STRENGTH

Hast thou not known? hast thou not heard, that the everlasting God, the LORD, the Creator of the ends of the earth, fainteth not, neither is weary? there is no searching of His understanding. He giveth power to the faint; and to them that have no might He increaseth strength. Even the youths shall faint and be weary, and the young men shall utterly fall: But they that wait upon the LORD shall renew their strength; they shall mount up with wings as eagles; they shall run, and not be weary; and they shall walk, and not faint.

And He said unto me, My grace is sufficient for thee: for My strength is made perfect in weakness. Most gladly therefore will I rather glory in my infirmities, that the power of Christ may rest upon me. Therefore I take pleasure in infirmities, in reproaches, in necessities, in persecutions, in distresses for Christ's sake: for when I am weak, then am I strong.

I can do all things through Christ which strengtheneth me.

Scripture References: Isaiah 40:28-31; 2 Corinthians 12:9-10; Philippians 4:13

A TRUE SISTER

A True Sister is a wonderful blessing from the Lord, because of her Love for you and her dedication to seeing you succeed in life.

Although at times she may not agree with you or may not understand why you do what you do, she never lets that stop her from loving you.

She is an active support system for you.

She will spend time with you and supply you with the resources that you need.

She is constantly pouring into your life, because she sees something in you and knows that her investment is not in vain.

She is Sweet. She is Witty. She is Funny.

She loves to make you laugh.

She is an Inspiration.

She is a Confidant and a Friend.

She is honest and frank with you.

She is your Wonderful Blessing from God.

KNOW YOUR WORTH

You are Fearfully and Wonderfully created by God. He does all things well and makes no mistakes. He has created you with purpose.

You are Bright, Intelligent, full of God's potential.

I stand in awe of His creation of you.

Walk towards your destiny in His Strength. Follow the path He has ordered for your steps, walking in His Word.

Be Virtuous, Gracious, a Woman of Prayer.

Trust Him in all and for all things.

Love others and love yourself, for you are a Woman of Great Worth.

You are God's Precious Jewel. He longs to continue to add facets to your life, so that you will shine more brilliantly. He wants His reflection of Himself in you to be perfected. Although the process may be painful, continue to allow the Master to add those facets.

Be encouraged and continue growing in Him!

He has anointed you to handle your life.

He always has your best interest at heart.

He loves you! Basque in His Everlasting Love!

YOU ARE ON HIS MIND

For I know the thoughts that I think toward you, saith the LORD, thoughts of peace, and not of evil, to give you an expected end. Then shall ye call upon Me, and ye shall go and pray unto Me, and I will hearken unto you. And ye shall seek Me, and find Me, when ye shall search for Me with all your heart. And I will be found of you, saith the LORD:

Jeremiah 29:11-14a

TO THE FATHERS

You are the divine covering for your family.

You protect, share wisdom, encourage, discipline, care for your family.

You can speak a word and things fall into order.

You are an example to your Sons on how to be men and to your Daughters on how a man should treat a woman.

Your love is strong, comforting and very precious.

Although you work hard throughout the week to provide for your family, do not forget to enjoy them. Make sure you spend quality time with them each and every precious moment you get.

Pour into their lives your wisdom, life experiences, encouragement and love. Always tell them and show them how much you care for them.

Your investment in their lives will produce a great legacy for you.

You make a difference in the lives of your family and the people you know.

TO THE MOTHERS

You are a

Unique

Beautiful

Precious

Priceless

JEWEL

Whose wonderful variety dazzles the eye.

Although at times all your hard work may seem to be unappreciated, and your responsibilities may sometimes cause you stress, know that you are loved and appreciated by the Heavenly Father.

He loves you with an unconditional love that you cannot even fathom.

So continue to press on and do what is right.

Make sure to always have some 'me time' and pamper yourself, so that you may be refreshed, as you continually give and pour out to others so much of yourself.

Be encouraged, my sister!

REMEMBER WHEN...

You held your baby in your arms with hopes and dreams for their future.

You took care of them when they were sick. You kissed the boo-boos and wiped their tears. You told them everything would be all right when they were afraid.

You took them to the places they needed to go. You were there for every important event.

You disciplined them when they needed it, because of your love for them.

You prayed for them and anointed them. You introduced them to Jesus. You taught them how to pray and prayed with them each day. You imparted God's Word and Wisdom to them.

You encouraged them when they were weary or doubting.

You supported them in their decisions. In Love, you let them know when you disagreed with them.

Your hard work has paid off and your labor was not in vain. Now they are grown, walking in the Faith that you shared with them, living out the hopes and dreams you had for them of an abundant life in Christ Jesus.

REJOICE NOW!

DO NOT FEAR

Fear thou not; for I am with thee: be not dismayed; for I am thy God: I will strengthen thee; yea, I will help thee; yea, I will uphold thee with the right hand of My righteousness.

No weapon that is formed against thee shall prosper; and every tongue that shall rise against thee in judgment thou shalt condemn. This is the heritage of the servants of the LORD, and their righteousness is of Me, saith the LORD.

For God hath not given us the spirit of fear; but of power, and of love, and of a sound mind.

There is no fear in love; but perfect love casteth out fear: because fear hath torment. He that feareth is not made perfect in love.

Scripture References: Isaiah 41:10; Isaiah 54:17; 2 Timothy 1:7; 1 John 4:18

DO NOT WORRY

Be careful for nothing; but in every thing by prayer and supplication with thanksgiving let your requests be made known unto God. And the peace of God, which passeth all understanding, shall keep your hearts and minds through Christ Jesus.

Therefore take no thought, saying, What shall we eat? or, What shall we drink? or, Wherewithal shall we be clothed? (For after all these things do the Gentiles seek:) for your heavenly Father knoweth that ye have need of all these things. But seek ye first the kingdom of God, and His righteousness; and all these things shall be added unto you.

Scripture References: Philippians 4:6-7; Matthew 6:31-33

CHANGING VENUES

As you progress onward to a new chapter in life,
always remember your foundation,

Jesus

Take Him with you wherever you go.

There will be times when it will look like the crowd
has it going on, but take a step back, assess the
situation, think and make a wise decision.

At times it is difficult to stand alone, but in the end you
will gain respect by living according to God's standard.

Be a rebel for Jesus

Follow Him

Share His goodness with others wherever you go!

A NEW THING

Remember ye not the former things, neither consider the things of old. Behold, I will do a new thing; now it shall spring forth; shall ye not know it? I will even make a way in the wilderness, and rivers in the desert.

Isaiah 43:18-19

CONTINUE

Continue to walk in the path that God has designed for you.

Continue to use the various gifts and talents that He has instilled in you for His glory.

Continue to strive for the things of God, and do not grow weary in your service for Him. Stand strong in Him. He will give you the strength to accomplish all that He has predestinated you to do in your life.

Rest in Him.

Continue to trust Him in all things.

Continue to grow in Him. Study His Word and get into His presence, so that He may continue to guide you.

Continue to do His will.

Continue to keep Him at the center of all you do.

Continue to be encouraged.

Continue to fall in love with Him each and every day, over and over and over again.

 CONTINUE!!!

TRUST AND HONOR HIM

Trust in the LORD with all thine heart; and lean not unto thine own understanding. In all thy ways acknowledge Him, and He shall direct thy paths. Be not wise in thine own eyes: fear the LORD, and depart from evil. It shall be health to thy navel, and marrow to thy bones. Honour the LORD with thy substance, and with the firstfruits of all thine increase: So shall thy barns be filled with plenty, and thy presses shall burst out with new wine.

Bring ye all the tithes into the storehouse, that there may be meat in Mine house, and prove Me now herewith, saith the LORD of hosts, if I will not open you the windows of heaven, and pour you out a blessing, that there shall not be room enough to receive it. And I will rebuke the devourer for your sakes, and he shall not destroy the fruits of your ground; neither shall your vine cast her fruit before the time in the field, saith the LORD of hosts. And all nations shall call you blessed: for ye shall be a delightsome land, saith the LORD of hosts.

Give, and it shall be given unto you; good measure, pressed down, and shaken together, and running over, shall men give into your bosom. For with the same measure that ye mete withal it shall be measured to you again.

Scripture References: Proverbs 3:5-10; Malachi 3:10-12; Luke 6:38

SUCCESSFUL LIVING

As we journey through this life, we have to pace ourselves alongside God's Divine timing. We have to be in tune with the Holy Spirit, He is the Lead of our life. He will teach us the ability to flow from season to season.

He will aid us in investigating our surroundings, give us discernment, show us that we need to take inventory of who is around us. Some will stay, placed at the forefront, the Exhorters, the Encouragers, the Cheerleaders, Those that tell you the Truth in Love, Those that have your best interest at heart, Those that you know, by their Fruit, tried the spirit by the Spirit, are your True Friends.

The others need to go or be placed in the background, no contact at all or not as much.

Many will say that they're your friend, but are really wolves in sheep's clothing. They are not really for you. Actions speak louder than words. At the first sign of blood or weakness, they will swoop down and try to take you out. They will attempt to tear you down and drain you dry.

True Friends exemplify the character of Christ. True Friends are Loyal. They Love you through the Good, the Bad, the Beautiful and the Ugly. They recognize that True Success is wrapped up in each other.

We need each other to survive.

We are not to think so highly of ourselves, but to help each other get to our appointed destinations in our journeys.

It's not about us. It's all about Jesus.

We are to use our Time, our Talents, our Gifts for the Kingdom.

If I can help somebody, that is Successful living.

DISCERNMENT

Beloved, believe not every spirit, but try the spirits whether they are of God: because many false prophets are gone out into the world. Hereby know ye the Spirit of God: Every spirit that confesseth that Jesus Christ is come in the flesh is of God: And every spirit that confesseth not that Jesus Christ is come in the flesh is not of God: and this is that spirit of antichrist, whereof ye have heard that it should come; and even now already is it in the world. Ye are of God, little children, and have overcome them: because greater is he that is in you, than he that is in the world.

1 John 4:1-4

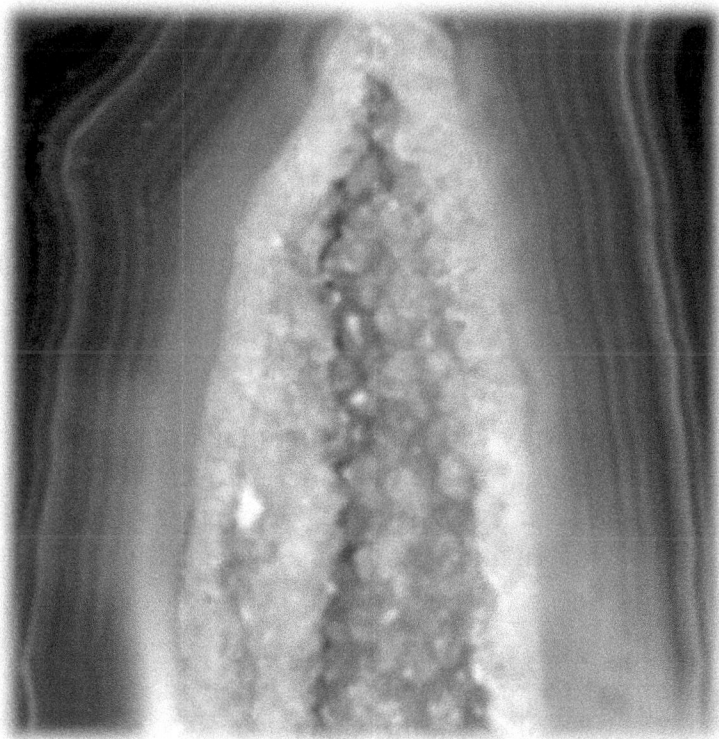

FRIENDSHIP

Do not take it lightly when a person allows you to be an important part of their life. If they have allowed you in, it shows a level of comfort that they feel with you.

Get to know one another and enjoy each other's company.

Learn when it is time to talk and when it is time to just be a listening ear.

As time progresses and trust is established, allow your conversations to go beyond the surface.

Be Transparent.

Be trustworthy with the information that they have imparted to you. Ask for permission to share what they have told you, if a situation arises that you know the information can help someone else.

Be Loyal.

Learn to love one another through the good, the bad, the beautiful and the ugly.

If you see your friend going astray, in LOVE, speak to them, restore them with the WORD, pray for them and with them.

Know that one of the purposes of your relationship is to pour into their life to enhance them.

Be an Encourager.

Let them know how wonderful they are and how they are so richly BLESSED by GOD.

Sow seeds of Kindness, Love, Patience.

Just as a beautiful garden requires tending to maintain its beauty, so do Friendships. Do the work and you each will reap a bountiful harvest.

LOSS

The loss of a loved one is a very saddening experience.

Walk through these days by facing one moment at a time.

Take the time to grieve.

As you heal, always keep your fond remembrances of them in your heart and mind.

Although they will not be there physically,

They are just a thought away...

POSITIVE THINKING

Finally, brethren, whatsoever things are true, whatsoever things are honest, whatsoever things are just, whatsoever things are pure, whatsoever things are lovely, whatsoever things are of good report; if there be any virtue, and if there be any praise, think on these things.

Philippians 4:8

THE UNBREAKABLE BOND

Who shall separate us from the love of Christ? shall tribulation, or distress, or persecution, or famine, or nakedness, or peril, or sword? As it is written, For Thy sake we are killed all the day long; we are accounted as sheep for the slaughter. Nay, in all these things we are more than conquerors through Him that loved us. For I am persuaded, that neither death, nor life, nor angels, nor principalities, nor powers, nor things present, nor things to come, Nor height, nor depth, nor any other creature, shall be able to separate us from the love of God, which is in Christ Jesus our Lord.

Romans 8:35-39

FAITH

I will stand upon my watch, and set me upon the tower, and will watch to see what He will say unto me, and what I shall answer when I am reproved. And the LORD answered me, and said, Write the vision, and make it plain upon tables, that he may run that readeth it. For the vision is yet for an appointed time, but at the end it shall speak, and not lie: though it tarry, wait for it; because it will surely come, it will not tarry. Behold, his soul which is lifted up is not upright in him: but the just shall live by his faith.

For we walk by faith, not by sight:

Now faith is the substance of things hoped for, the evidence of things not seen.

But without faith it is impossible to please Him: for he that cometh to God must believe that He is, and that He is a rewarder of them that diligently seek Him.

Scripture References: Habakkuk 2:1-4;
2 Corinthians 5:7; Hebrews 11:1;
Hebrews 11:6

IMPARTATION

You are the Son, the Daughter, of the Most High GOD!

You are Special. You are Loved.

God has a wonderful plan for your life.

You will do great and mighty things.

Set goals for your life.

You can achieve whatever you put your Faith to do.

Pursue your dreams. Dream big, because God has limitless resources. Never let age or circumstances hold you back. God will supply all your need according to His riches in Glory.

Be an encouragement to others. Love them in spite of. Be a Blessing to them. Invest in their lives.

Be there for those God has assigned you to.

Have Faith in God. Encourage yourself with His WORD.

Walk in your Faith.

Always have hope. Put your expectations in Him.

He never fails!

ASSURANCE

Being confident of this very thing, that He which hath begun a good work in you will perform it until the day of Jesus Christ:

Commit thy works unto the LORD, and thy thoughts shall be established.

Humble yourselves therefore under the mighty hand of God, that He may exalt you in due time: Casting all your care upon Him; for He careth for you.

And let us not be weary in well doing: for in due season we shall reap, if we faint not.

Trust in the LORD, and do good; so shalt thou dwell in the land, and verily thou shalt be fed. Delight thyself also in the LORD: and He shall give thee the desires of thine heart. Commit thy way unto the LORD; trust also in Him; and He shall bring it to pass.

Now unto Him that is able to do exceeding abundantly above all that we ask or think, according to the power that worketh in us, Unto Him be glory in the church by Christ Jesus throughout all ages, world without end. Amen.

Scripture References: *Philippians 1:6; Proverbs 16:3; 1 Peter 5:6-7; Galatians 6:9; Psalm 37:3-5; Ephesians 3:20-21*

ABOUT THE AUTHOR

Tracey Payton Younger was born and raised in Philadelphia, Pennsylvania. She truly loves and is in love with her Lord and Savior, Jesus Christ. She has always possessed a spirit of creativity and imagination. As a young child, she exhibited talent in various areas of the Arts, Singing, Acting, and Dancing, which her family honed via involving her in the choirs and the Drama Ministry at their church and enrolling her into dancing school. As she matured, more talents began to surface in other areas, Poetry, Song, Story and Script Writing, Abstract Drawing, Arts and Crafts, Photography and Videography. Her passion is to serve the Lord and to aid others on their journey through life.

www.ingramcontent.com/pod-product-compliance
Lightning Source LLC
Chambersburg PA
CBHW072039060426
42449CB00010BA/2354